BEHIND
THE
LEGEND

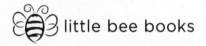 little bee books

An imprint of Bonnier Publishing USA

251 Park Avenue South, New York, NY 10010

Copyright © 2017 by Bonnier Publishing USA

All rights reserved, including the right of reproduction in whole or in part in any form.

LITTLE BEE BOOKS is a trademark of Bonnier Publishing USA, and associated colophon is a trademark of Bonnier Publishing USA.

Manufactured in the United States LB 0817

Names: Peabody, Erin, author. | Rivas, Victor, illustrator.
Title: Werewolves / by Erin Peabody; illustrated by Victor Rivas.
Description: New York City: Little Bee Books, 2017. | Series: Behind the legend
Identifiers: LCCN 2016047315| Subjects: LCSH: Werewolves—Juvenile literature.
Classification: LCC GR830.W4 P43 2017 | DDC 398.24/54—dc23
LC record available at https://lccn.loc.gov/2016047315

ISBN 978-1-4998-0459-1 (hc)
First Edition 10 9 8 7 6 5 4 3 2 1
ISBN 978-1-4998-0458-4 (pbk)
First Edition 10 9 8 7 6 5 4 3 2 1

littlebeebooks.com
bonnierpublishingusa.com

WEREWOLVES

by Erin Peabody

art by Victor Rivas

little bee books

CONTENTS

INTRODUCTION

MEET THE MONSTER

"Even a man who is pure in heart
and says his prayers by night
may become a wolf when the wolfbane blooms
and the autumn moon is bright."
—Quote from 1941 movie *The Wolf Man*

Victims say it starts with a trembling. Uncontrollable tremors and tics seize the body. Bones, including the spine, twist and bend, inflicting tremendous pain. Thick, dark hairs sprout up all over the skin, even on the hands, feet, and face.

Next, teeth sharpen. Claws like switchblades spring from the fingertips. Normal breathing escalates to a heavy pant. Finally, and most horrifically, the afflicted is overwhelmed by an oppressive, unshakable thirst for blood.

Fully transformed, a werewolf emerges: a human now possessed with the most deplorable and unthinkable beastly urges.

There are some people who claim to have experienced such a monstrous metamorphosis. The physical changes are so horribly painful, they say, that witnesses have described hearing terrifying groans and screams in the proximity of the person being transformed.

Then there's the loss of control—often instigated by the hypnotizing glow of a full moon or powerful emotions, like anger, boiling over. The primal urge to hunt, strike, or even kill also takes hold, with some victims conjuring all the willpower and good conscience they possess to try and tame the raging impulses.

It's hard to imagine a more horrific experience. But just where did werewolves—or at least our concept of them—come from? Is it possible that humans could really morph into these hairy beasts?

And, above all else, are werewolves real? The answers, drawn largely from ancient stories and reports, appear in the following pages. They'll likely leave you howling in terror and laughter—and possibly, thinking more about your own inner wolf.

CHAPTER ONE
ANCIENT TAILS

"... my face became monstrous, my nostrils wide ... mine ears rugged with hair ..." —A shape-shifting beast from an ancient Roman novel by Apuleius

The werewolf has haunted the collective human mind for hundreds of years. It's one of our oldest and most feared monsters, known even as far back as Julius Caesar's time, in the first century BCE. The prospect of a ruthless half man, half wolf lurking in the woods, countryside, or village tormented not just our ancestors, but our ancestors' ancestors, too.

The hybrid beast was so feared and loathed that those suspected of unleashing such terror were punished brutally. People accused of being werewolves were burned at the stake or forced to endure other forms of barbaric torture that are simply too horrific to mention!

But, if we journey back in time to stories of the earliest humans, we learn that the notion of werewolves, like other "were-beasts," was actually quite common. In some cases, the transformation was even seen as positive and enlightening.

"CH-CH-CHANGES..."

The word *wer*, in Old English, means man. Hence the word *werewolf* means, most literally, man-wolf. Across numerous cultures, people have believed in the idea of shape-shifting—turning from one animal into another, or at least, assuming one or more of its qualities, traits, or abilities.

In Norse mythology, the mischievous god Loki, for instance, transforms himself into a whole assortment of animals, including such fascinating creatures as a horse, a seal, and a salmon. He also turns into a fly. Odd choice, Loki.

In ancient Egypt, a part man, part jackal named Anubis was a revered god. A popular Egyptian image, this deity with a doglike head was thought to guard the dead during the burial process and prepare them for the afterlife.

"Weretigers" and "werefoxes" were known across China and Japan. In the South American country of Chile, it was believed that witches transformed into *chonchon*, vulture-like birds that flew through dark forests at night.

Native American tribes, though quite diverse in their beliefs and customs, cherish many stories focused on animal spirits and shape-shifting. Animals such as the bear, eagle, and wolf are popular figures representing such virtues as wisdom, strength, and loyalty. A young hunter, for instance, might mimic the clever and stealthy wolf in hopes of improving his hunting skills.

Numerous other examples of were-animals exist across the world's diverse cultures. Such creatures have included serpents, leopards, lions, panthers, coyotes, buffalo, owls, sharks, and crocodiles. And according to one old legend? Hedgehogs.

ANIMAL POWERS

Long ago, many cultures believed that there was a much finer line between human and beast than most of us think. Animals were studied, mimicked, and even worshiped for the positive qualities they possessed. An eagle, for instance, might have been revered for its keen vision, a cheetah for its speed, and a dog for its loyalty.

What if you could shape-shift into an animal? What creature would you choose and why?

THE DARK SIDE

So, at what point, you might be wondering, did shape-shifting turn into something fearsome and freaky? Where did the werewolf go wrong? When did it become the fanged, bloodthirsty monster that looms so large in pop culture today?

As we often do, let's look to history's imaginative and prolific storytellers, the Greeks, for answers. In their ancient writings, we can find one of the earliest werewolf stories ever written.

According to accounts by the ancient Greek writer Pausanias, who was born way back in 110 CE, and the ancient Roman Ovid, the hairy tale centers on the god Zeus and his growing disgust with humanity.

(Apparently, we humans have always had issues.) The mighty Zeus decides to visit the world of mortals disguised as a peasant so that he can get an even closer look (for some reason!) at mankind's ugly flaws.

Zeus's negative opinions about people are sadly confirmed. He continues to witness more greed, selfishness, and violence. But no event aggravates his fiery tempers more than his visit with the imperious King Lycaon of Arcadia. The ruler, an "inhospitable tyrant" according to one version of the story, mocks Zeus even *after* learning of the god's true identity. Then, in a most gruesome insult, Lycaon serves Zeus a dinner that includes—

gag alert!—a boiled person! Enraged, the king of all gods summons his showstopping thunderbolts to destroy Lycaon's palace and deliver justice.

As for Lycaon himself, he's doomed to live the remainder of his days as the bloodthirsty beast he most resembles: a wolf. He tries desperately to speak, to protest his mangy, four-legged condition, but all he can do is hooowwwl. . . .

King Lycaon was not given his name by accident. That's because *lyc* means wolf in Greek. The unpopular ruler was named after the wolf, presumably because of his savage ways and penchant for human dinner entrees.

Lyc is also the basis for words like lycanthropy, a medical condition in which a person believes he or she is really a wolf. And if you want to sound clever, a lycanthrope is just another word for werewolf.

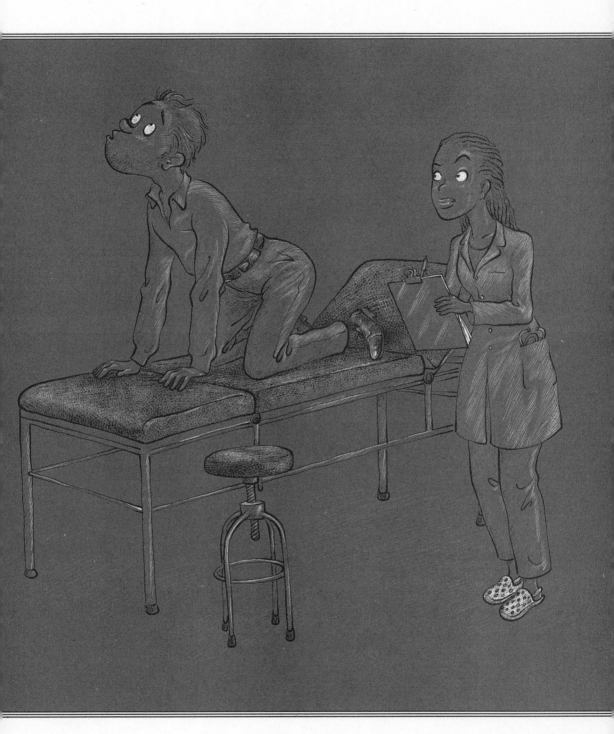

BIG, BAD WOLF

Based on this story, you can see how some cultures came to loathe and fear the wolf. Over time, we saddled it with humankind's most despicable qualities, including greediness and ruthlessness. The wolf, you might say, became humanity's scapegoat. Talk about some interesting shape-shifting!

Evil and cunning, the wolf prowls throughout our oldest fairy tales and legends. You've undoubtedly heard many of these stories, which have been around since the sixteenth and seventeenth centuries. There's *Little Red Riding Hood*, *The Three Little Pigs*, *Peter and the Wolf*, and to some degree, *Beauty and the Beast*. Can you think of others?

Wolves have dug their claws deeply into our imaginations. They've played a leading role in fiction—tales, myths, and legends—across history. But what about werewolves—the idea of a man, woman, or even child, physically turning into a wolf? This is a person not just acting beastly, but literally becoming one. Could such a terrible transformation really happen?

Let's start our investigation into this question in the German countryside, not far from where the Brothers Grimm once penned their own tales about a big, bad wolf.

CHAPTER TWO

OF WOLVES AND THE WICKED

"Give me raw meat. I am a wolf, a wolf!"—Man from nineteenth-century Europe who believed he was a werewolf

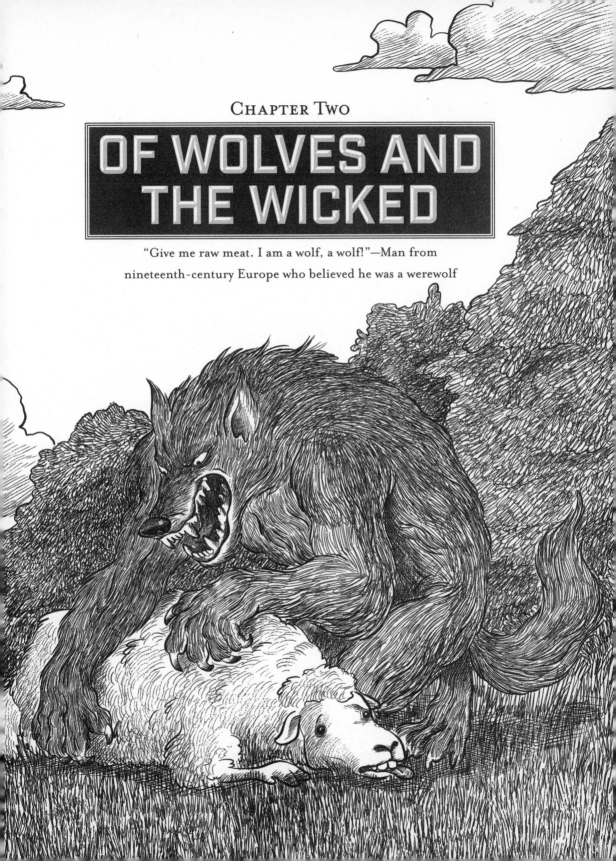

In the mid-sixteenth century, in the little German town of Bedburg near Cologne, a savage, gruesome killer was on the loose. At first, the victims were mostly small livestock. Farmers would wake up in the morning and find that one of their lambs or goats was missing. The only thing that remained would be splatters of blood. Other times, horribly, the farmers would find remnants of the animals, which had been mutilated, torn apart, or half eaten.

Over time, it became clear that the killing wasn't limited to livestock. Men and women were also found murdered. Detached arms and legs were discovered on dark village streets and on pathways in the woods. Children vanished without a trace.

In one instance, a young girl was playing with friends on a small farm in the village when a beast appeared out of nowhere. It struck swiftly, lunging at her throat. Fortunately, her coat saved her. Its stiff, high collar acted as a shield surrounding her small neck.

But the beast wasn't finished. He continued to leap and pounce among the group of children who ran about frantically, screaming and wailing. Thank goodness for the nearby cattle. The chaos spooked them so much that they banded together and charged the savage invader, who fled. The children were safe, at least for now.

A CREEP IN WOLF'S CLOTHING

For twenty-five years, the fear of this "insatiable bloodsucker," as one report described it, terrorized the residents of Bedburg. Leaders in town organized a massive hunt, releasing packs of dogs to sniff out and destroy the grisly menace.

Finally, one autumn day in 1589, hunters closed in on their target. As many had suspected, the brutal, barbaric killer turned out to be a wolf. Or was it? According to a centuries-old report, just as the beast was being captured, it threw aside an unusual belt. The hunters just stared in amazement. The creature they'd ensnared was not a wolf at all—but a man, a villager everyone in town knew: Peter Stubb.

As you can imagine, witnesses were shaken and shocked to learn that a person they knew, and perhaps saw on a daily basis, could be responsible for such despicable crimes. Right away, Stubb was arrested and brought to trial.

He was tortured on the rack, a machine used to literally stretch a person—one of several practices of punishment common during the medieval period. Unable to tolerate the pain any more, Stubb admitted to being a werewolf. He confessed to murdering and cannibalizing at least sixteen people, victims he allegedly described as "dainty morsels." He also explained that he derived his magical, transformative powers from a magic girdle, or belt, given to him by the Devil.

He was put to death on October 31, 1589, by having his flesh poked with red-hot burning pincers.

CHARMED TOOLS

The story of Peter Stubb is horrific. But one aspect that's hard not to laugh at is the notion of a magic girdle. Really? A girdle? Like the kind your great-grandmother might have worn? Yet, according to lore, such tangible objects were employed—with all seriousness—to help induce a wolf transformation.

The girdle was likely a portion of wolf skin or a pelt worn around the waist. Donning an animal's fur, feathers, teeth, or other body parts was thought to convey certain powers or traits to the person wearing them. Some individuals also believed that special ointments made from herbs and plants could be rubbed on the body to induce "wolfy" changes.

BEDEVILED

Stubb blamed his horrendous acts on the Devil (a very common, yet cowardly, cop out in the Middle Ages). While his case was extraordinarily gruesome, Stubb wasn't the only werewolf in history to be linked to dark and evil forces. There have been others, and many possess a common thread among them: magic.

This magic, however, is not the sparkly good kind that sometimes seems responsible for the inexplicable happy stuff in our lives. No, werewolf magic is dark magic—full of curses, spells, voodoo dolls, and more. For example, dark magic, or black magic, is the kind that Harry Potter is always battling against. Black magic is to blame for one very dark story in werewolf lore. Its main characters involved werewolves and children—or, more specifically, *werewolf children*.

WOMEN GET WOLFISH

Historical accounts of werewolves aren't only stories about men being transformed. Several cases also involve women stricken with a wolf-like rage. One of the best-known tales features a married woman in 1558 in France.

According to a "reliable source," says the old account, the story starts when the woman's husband asks a passing huntsman if he'd be willing to share some meat with the couple. The hunter agrees but says he must catch something first. He sets out into the woods near the couple's small cottage to look for game.

It isn't long before an enormous wolf lunges at him. The hunter shoots at the creature, but it remains unfazed. When the wolf leaps at him again, the man ultimately fights it off with only a knife and his bare hands. He's able to slice off the animal's paw, which makes the beast finally retreat.

Rattled, the hunter dashes back to the cottage to relate the frightful ordeal. He reaches into his pocket to show the cottage owner the wolf's paw, proof of his unusual confrontation. But he pulls out something else instead: a woman's hand, adorned with a wedding ring that looks strangely familiar. . . . The cottage dweller runs to fetch his wife. He finds her hiding her hand beneath her apron. When he grabs at her concealed arm, he sees that she's missing a hand.

Accused of sorcery and witchcraft, the woman is promptly put to death.

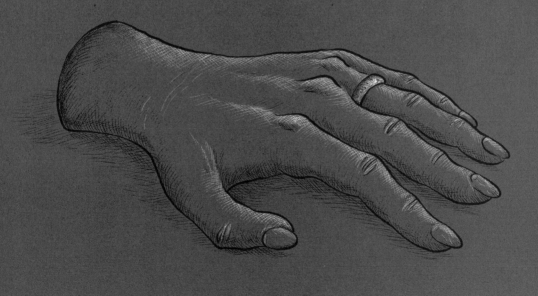

CHAPTER THREE

"OUI, OUI," SAID THE WEREWOLF

"For this was the land of the ever-memorable Beast, the
Napoleon Bonaparte of wolves." —Robert Louis Stevenson
during an 1878 journey through France

D epending on your taste in things like movies, fiction books, and Halloween costumes, this news will either thrill you . . . or totally freak you out: There have been kids, according to some historical accounts, who have been transformed into werewolves. And these little monsters weren't the furry kind with removable plastic fangs. Far from it: They were snarling, savage beasts who committed terrifying acts.

One well-known tale about creepy kiddos took place in France, in the sixteenth century (or 1500s, if you will). It started with a young girl named Pernette Gandillon who was so convinced she was a wolf that she ran around howling on all fours.

One day, instead of playing as most children do, Pernette was on the prowl, hunting for her next target. Suddenly, she came upon a sight that her inner monster couldn't resist: two gentle-looking children, a brother and sister, out picking strawberries.

It's hard to imagine, but as the very old tale goes, Pernette, overcome by dark and barbaric forces, pounced on the girl. Hardly the meek sort, the siblings fought back—and fiercely. They endured many nasty scratches, but thankfully, were able to chase off their crazed attacker, although the brother died shortly after. Pernette was pointed out by the lone survivor and was immediately killed by a mob of townspeople.

BROTHER WOLF

Pernette may have been gone, but another sinister wolf soon emerged from the same pack: her brother, Pierre. The boy claimed that a magical ointment helped transform him into a werewolf. He was also said to nibble on the raw flesh of small mammals and to pal around with witches. And later on, a grown-up Pierre's children committed equally disturbing deeds. His son Georges, also an admitted werewolf, once claimed to have attacked and killed two goats. And Pierre's daughter admitted to being a witch.

As you can imagine, villagers were terrified of the craven clan that threatened to spoil their nice little French town, which was otherwise, presumably, full of good things like baguettes, fine cheese, and chocolates. (For whatever reason, werewolves plagued the country of the Eiffel Tower in the fifteenth and sixteenth centuries. You'll hear about other Frenchie fiends later on.)

As for Pierre and Georges, locals were convinced that the two were werewolves, even though the family members wouldn't fully admit this until they were captured. The evidence, as villagers saw it, were the numerous scars, in the form of bites and scratches, that covered their bodies. Supposedly, the father and son duo received the wounds when they were in werewolf form and were attacked by packs of dogs sent out to hunt them.

In the end, a mounting fear of more vicious attacks put an end to Pierre and his menacing children. Just like their victims, they died a brutal and barbaric death at the hands of their accusers.

MORE FEAR IN FRANCE

We'll now fast-forward about two hundred years to the south-central region of France known at one time as Gévaudan. This location allegedly suffered one of the longest-running and most violent werewolf episodes in history. For almost three years, people there lived in nearly perpetual panic, fearing a vicious creature that preyed on the innocent.

It started in the summer of 1764 when a young woman was outdoors tending to her cattle. Suddenly a strange beast lunged at her. Sensing danger, the cattle instantly banded together and charged at the creature. (Who knew cows could be so heroic?) Large bulls in the herd thrust their horns at the invader. Fortunately, all the back-and-forth jousting gave the woman a chance to escape.

Others, however, weren't so lucky. Men, but mostly women and children, were also mercilessly attacked. It's believed that in a period of just one week, four people were besieged and eaten.

"WOLF-ENA"?

The beast was swift and elusive, but eventually, enough eyewitness accounts were gathered to form a good description of the monster. According to a poster printed in 1764, it looked like a cross between a wolf and a hyena. It also possessed a "long gaping jaw, six claws, pointy upright ears and a supple furry tail. . . ."

Eventually a name was given to this horrid monster. They called it La Bête du Gévaudan. *La bête*, as you French-speaking students may know, means beast.

Not the most original or descriptive name! A more fitting and frightening description of the creature showed up in *London Magazine* in 1765. According to the article, the beast's teeth were "most formidable," and its powerful, long tail dealt "swinging blows." The animal, it went on, "vaulted to tremendous heights, and ran with supernatural speed."

One more thing: the creature's smell "was beyond description."

At one point, villagers estimated that the fiend was responsible for one hundred deaths. Fighting efforts were scaled up. Packs of bloodhound dogs were released to track down the horrid savage. Hunting parties, composed of the best shooters in the area, fanned out across the region's meadows and forests. All tried desperately to track the beast down. Some even spotted it and got off clean shots at it. But none were successful in bringing it down. The brute, so clever it seemed, always managed to lope off or limp away, leaving only more bloodshed in its wake.

As fear in Gévaudan hit a fever pitch, King Louis XV in Versailles couldn't help but take notice. The panic was becoming a political

issue—one that could leave his people vulnerable to war or invasion. So, he posted large rewards to anyone who could kill the dreaded beast. This drew armies of men, some with upwards of 20,000 people, who joined in the battle against the monster.

Deadly poison was also enlisted. Carcasses of small animals were laced with poison and left as bait. Yet, none of these tactics worked. The efforts only led to more deaths. Sadly, many domestic animals and livestock fed on the tainted bait traps and died, as did around 1,000 innocent wolves. The beast responsible for the carnage, however, remained unscathed.

Superstitious townspeople were now convinced that the invincible animal was a sorcerer, a werewolf that magically defied people's efforts to destroy it. One farmer claimed he'd even heard this half man, half wolf speaking.

THE BEST SHOT

Another hunting party was organized, this time led by an experienced gun carrier for the king, Antoine Beauterne. He carefully studied the beast and the terrain it roamed.

One day, after he and his men had infiltrated the area where the beast was last seen, the party's dogs started barking wildly. They howled relentlessly until they'd flushed the creature out. Beauterne immediately shot at it. The expert gunman's bullet struck the beast's head, passing right through it. Still, the fierce brute rose up, enduring additional bullets, as it had so many times before. But this time, there were simply too many. With Beauterne's men repeatedly discharging their weapons at it, the long-feared killer finally collapsed for good.

Accounts say that upon close examination, the epic creature was an exceptionally large wolf, weighing over 140 pounds. Eventually, hunters tracked down and killed a second wolf-like beast similar to it, which was thought responsible for many of the deaths, too. Hunters tried to preserve at least one of the beast's bodies, but they were unsuccessful. By the time the carcass reached the king, it had started to decompose, causing great offense to his royal highness.

The lack of a good, preserved specimen also robs us of answers today. Modern scientists would be keenly interested in learning about the possibility of such a strange hybrid beast, if it in fact truly existed.

THEORIES, BUT NO ANSWERS

Modern researchers have a couple of theories about the Beast of Gévaudan. Maybe it was merely a pack of different wolves, or possibly it was an animal unknown to science, perhaps a wolf-dog hybrid?

Others, in digging through the records of people alive in Gévaudan at the time, suspect the creature could have been a hyena.

A local at the time, Antoine Chastel, was thought to have a collection of exotic animals that he caged in a menagerie at his French residence. (Menageries, showy displays of unusual wildlife, were popular among kings and the wealthy.)

Could one or more of these animals have escaped and caused the horrible slaughtering of people? And there's another theory. Could this man, or another member of his family, have trained the beast(s) to attack? More than one witness, old records show, insist that they saw a man alongside the beast.

Who knows what kind of creature, or man, might have been responsible for the horrible deaths in France so long ago? Was the animal a wilder, more primitive precursor to today's wolves? Or was the attacker an imported hyena, trained by men to commit atrocious acts? Or, lastly, was the beast really a werewolf: part man and part beast? Perhaps someday, more evidence will surface to help reveal the truth about this eighteenth-century mystery.

CHAPTER FOUR

TODAY'S BEAST

"Better stay away from him. He'll rip your lungs out, Jim."
—Lyrics from a 1978 song, "Werewolves of London"

So far, we've explored history's most famous wolfish brutes. Many, like Peter Stubb and the Gandillon siblings, were supposedly motivated by dark and sinister forces. The Beast of Gévaudan, on the other hand, presented its own unique case. Perhaps it was a bloodthirsty hyena or a trained killing beast.

But what of our modern werewolf? The panting, wild-eyed beast we know from books, films, and cartoons that can't help but sprout thick hair and bark at the moon? We'll explore this bizarre man/beast hybrid in this chapter. We'll also learn how just a couple of decades ago, a mysterious midnight rambler spooked an American town.

WAYS OF THE WOLF

All werewolf believers contend that these howling beasts have certain qualities in common. Physically, there's of course the thick fur that covers the body, including on the hands, feet, and face. A werewolf's ears become pointed and alert. Its canine teeth grow longer and sharper—as do its claws, which are now thought capable of scaling walls, trees, and the sides of buildings. Its energy, speed, and strength become boundless.

POINTED EARS

THICK HAIR

SHARP TEETH

STRONG MUSCLES

POWERFUL CLAWS

BAD BROWS

According to ancient myth and some modern-day werewolf believers, thick eyebrows, particularly those that grow closely together, are a sign that someone might have werewolf or vampire tendencies. As far back as the Greeks, thick "unibrows" as we kiddingly call them, have been associated with bad luck, immortality, and a violent temper.

Of course, there's absolutely no evidence to back up this ridiculous contention! The only explanation might be that the shape of our eyebrows, affected by our facial expressions when we're happy, angry, or sad, can dramatically alter how we look.

For instance, many fictional cartoon villains, like the Evil Queen in *Snow White*, possess severely arched eyebrows as a way of conveying a cruel and menacing demeanor.

Behaviorally, there are changes, too, even bigger ones. The individual's personality is consumed, lost to the inner, more primitive beast. Entranced, he or she becomes a hunter, hungry for the taste of fresh blood and flesh.

These changes are thought to be voluntary, or involuntary. The powerful pull of the moon, a curse, or spell are believed to overpower an innocent person and induce a transformation. And according to many modern books and movies, becoming a werewolf can also be as easy—and unfortunate—as catching a cold! In this case, the werewolf spreads his "disease" via a bite, or genetically passes it on to his offspring or other descendants. Other modern werewolf believers claim that willpower alone, or the willful use of black magic, can affect a "wolfy" transformation.

Perhaps you love werewolves. Maybe that's why you reached for this book. But did you know that werewolf lore has so invaded our own modern culture that it's inspired everything from books, movies, and songs to toys, costumes, ice cream flavors, and candy? Ever nibbled on "werewolf fur"? Don't fear; it's *only* brown cotton candy. . . .

Even if you're not a believer—you loathe full moons and are decidedly vegetarian—you can still get a laugh, or a shiver, from pop culture's extensive werewolf offerings. There are endless fiction book options that feature the fanged creatures: from Scooby-Doo and the Goosebumps series to the Harry Potter series, and, of course, the Twilight series.

Several songs across the genres and decades have also been inspired by wolfish tones, and include: "We Bite," "I Was a Teenage Werewolf," "Bark at the Moon," and "Werewolf Blues." As for playthings, there are werewolf Legos and numerous figurines. There's candy, perfect for Halloween, including werewolf gummies and mints in the shape of werewolf-slaying silver bullets. And if you feel brave enough to play the part, costume accessories abound, from werewolf ears, feet, toenails, and claws, to stick-on fur, tails, and customized fangs. (My, what large canines you have!) You can even dress up your little brother or sister, or better yet, your dog or cat!

A MIDWEST MONSTER

In the late 1980s and early '90s, a wicked creature reportedly prowled across southeast Wisconsin. According to eyewitnesses, it was wolf-like, at least six feet tall, and had pointed ears, slanted eyes, and hairy, clawed, humanlike hands.

At first the reports were scattered and considered mostly the product of overly imaginative local teens. Then, a local writer and cartoonist started to publish the accounts. More and more stories flooded in, many containing the same disturbing details.

In many instances, people encountered the strange beast while out driving the country roads near Elkhorn, Wisconsin. Specifically, the reports occurred along or near Bray Road, leading locals to call the spooky brute the Beast of Bray Road.

STAY IN YOUR CAR

Witnesses spied it creeping along the side of the road. Sometimes it was gripping meat in its wolfish hands. Other times it was pawing at roadkill. Still, other eyewitnesses were distraught by the strange, uncanny look in its eyes. They were convinced the beast was staring at them with an evil glare and a smirk-like look on its face.

In 1990, three children out sledding believed they saw it. It was covered in thick, scraggly, silver-gray hair, they recalled, and standing on two legs. After taking a few awkward steps, it went down on all four legs and bolted toward them. It chased them for about 250 yards, then, suddenly distracted, it took off in another direction. According to the kids, who got a close-up view of their pursuer, the animal had a wolf's head, a man's neck, and a dog-like body.

Fortunately, no one was injured or killed at the hands (or paws) of this mysterious wolf-like beast. Others in the region claimed it charged at them, but they were never hurt. Which brings up an interesting topic: What should you do if a werewolf were to attack you?

SURVIVOR'S GUIDE TO . . . WEREWOLVES?

Even as kids, you've been drilled on how to escape a lot of stressful situations, including fires, downed airplanes, and in some cases, tornadoes, hurricanes, earthquakes, and monsoons, too. [Your bravery, by the way, is commendable.]

But what about a fanged monster coming for your throat? The chances are slight, undoubtedly, that this would ever, *ever* happen to you. But according to werewolf believers, there are a few things you can do to drive away a crazed human/wolf:

• Say its human name.

• Tap its forehead three times. [Of course, disregard this if the werewolf is trying to eat you!]

• The ultimate no-fail trick: Shoot it with a silver bullet. (However, this is *much* too complicated and dangerous for kids. Consider it only an FYI.)

• Finally, if nothing else works, present it with roses. (P.S. This is known to work wonders across numerous human conflicts, especially those involving girls!)

So what do we make of the Beast of Bray Road? Is the creature a true wolfman on the prowl some place right now in the cornfields of Wisconsin?

Likely not, say experts. The monster, like Bigfoot and other popular cryptids, is likely just a misidentified creature—such as a coyote, large dog, wolf, or some other animal. Many of the episodes described by eyewitnesses happened at night, in the dark, when one's vision was unclear or comprised. Combine this with a primal fear of wild wolves and beasts and you can see how monsters like the Beast of Bray Road are born.

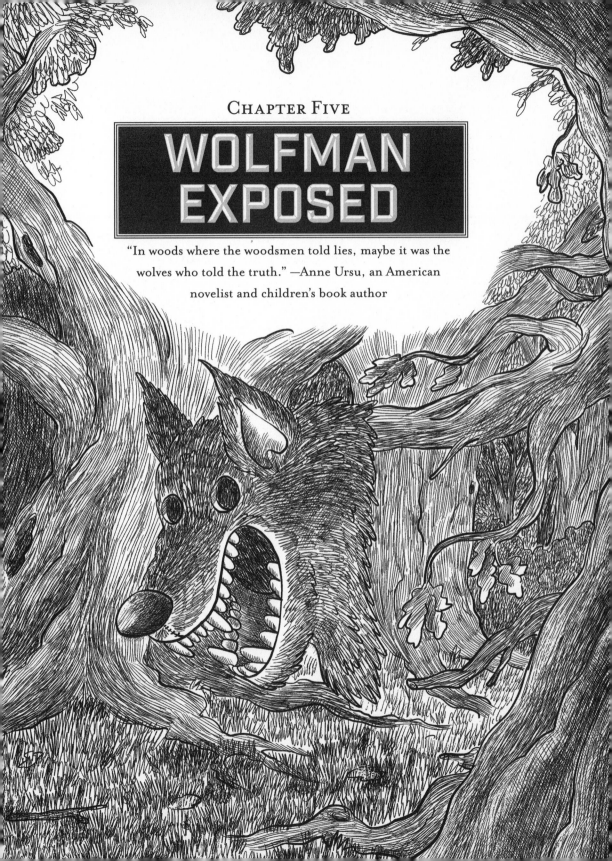

CHAPTER FIVE

WOLFMAN EXPOSED

"In woods where the woodsmen told lies, maybe it was the wolves who told the truth." —Anne Ursu, an American novelist and children's book author

I n the preceding pages, we've explored a lot of grisly werewolf accounts across history. You've read about the most horrible acts allegedly committed by half-person, half-wolf beasts.

Sometimes these despicable monsters, as centuries-old texts tell us, were motivated by evil, dark forces. Other times the creatures were thought to be wild animals with a strange penchant for attacking and killing human beings.

Some of the stories or details you've read may seem far-fetched. For instance, why did it take the people of Gévaudan three years to stop a beast that had killed around one hundred people? Could a little girl, like Pernette Gandillon, and her brother really turn into wolves? What caused them to act in such cruel and unusual ways?

Such critical thinking is helpful in solving any number of problems, as well as parsing apart ancient legends and myths. And it's exactly the kind of thing that good investigators do.

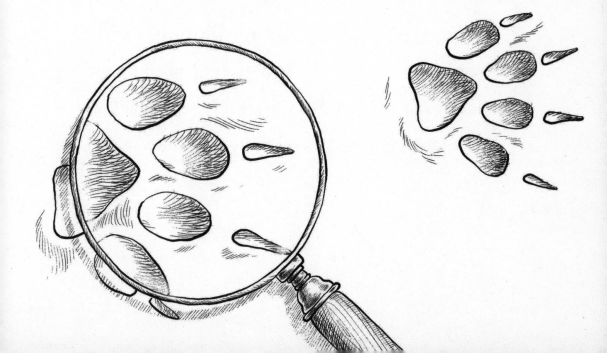

A MICROSCOPE ON THE MANGY

Let's examine werewolf transformation first. While it's been described by several individuals, particularly those living a *very* long time ago, there is simply no evidence that such a complex, powerful process has ever happened. There is not a single photo or video anywhere in existence showing a person undergoing such a terrible transformation.

So why would anyone propose such a thing happening? What's the basis for all of those old stories and tales? Well, here are a few explanations offered up by experts, especially historians.

The first explanation regards mental illness. From the sixteenth to the nineteenth centuries, society had a very poor understanding and perception of mental health issues. (In fact, you could argue the same thing today! Although, lucky for us, medical knowledge is SO much more advanced.)

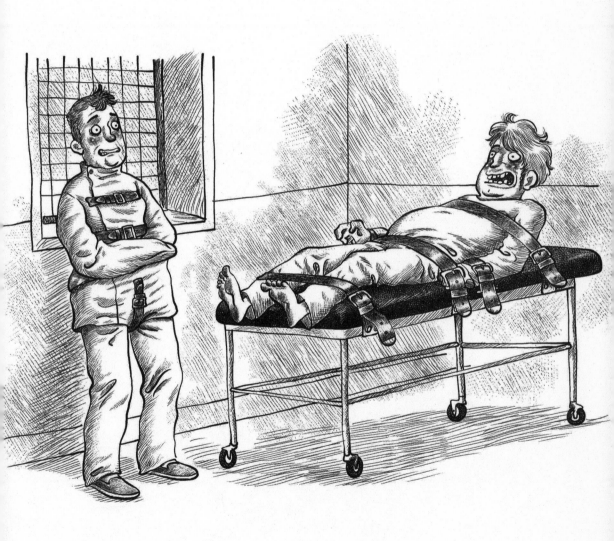

Centuries ago, mentally ill people were shunned, despised, even demonized. When individuals became uncontrollably violent, they were often considered to be evil or possessed. They were seen as aligned with witches and werewolves, which also meant that they were often imprisoned—or worse, tortured for their hapless conditions.

MOLDY GRAIN

Hallucinations, induced by poor food supplies, are another explanation. Centuries ago, people didn't know that grain could become infested with a fungus that was toxic enough to kill them. Ergot poisoning, as it's called, not only has the ability to make people physically sick, but it can also cause convulsions, delusions, and a sensation of one's skin crawling. Miserable, huh?

You can imagine then how someone displaying such bizarre symptoms in historical times might have been misunderstood. They were often considered crazed and maniacal. It's also quite possible that they were then accused of being werewolves or witches.

In fact, this idea was first proposed by behavioral psychologist Linnda Caporael in the 1970s when she was researching the Salem witch trials of 1692. She was the first to propose that contaminated grain, not witchcraft at all, might have been the reason several young women were accused of "witchy" behavior. Sadly, her explanation came centuries too late. Many of the accused witches around Salem, Massachusetts, were executed by hanging.

LONGTIME VILLAN

People can be misunderstood. So can animals. And no species has been more maligned than the wolf. As was discussed earlier, the caricature of the Big Bad Wolf prowls its way through countless fairy tales and historical works of fiction.

The carnivorous wolf can certainly be problematic—even today. This apex predator can destroy small livestock and cost farmers profits. But for whatever reason, centuries ago, disgust and fear about wolves became as potent as a disease. Wild and irrational stories were spun about bloodthirsty wolves that snuck into homes and stole children from their beds. (By the way, this has NEVER happened!)

The same hyped fears led villagers across England, Germany, and France to destroy wolves as quickly as they could shoot, poison, or trap them. By the eighteenth century, the entire species had been wiped out across all three countries.

People hated wolves so much that they associated them mostly with savagery and ruthlessness. Then, connections were drawn between humans that seemed barbaric and wolves themselves. Before long, stories and legends spread, including those

about werewolves. Religion and politics stoked people's fears, too, leading them to add only more chapters to the book of wicked wolf tales.

Many of the fairy tales are laughable, but the stereotypes about wolves that they sparked still rage on. The truth is, as you may already know, wolves are incredibly intelligent animals with a fascinating social structure. They are key predators, vital to many diverse habitats around the world.

CLOSE TIES

Perhaps most compelling is the connection between modern wolves and our favorite tail-wagging friends: dogs. Both share the same ancient wolf ancestry. Most scientists think that at some point, likely fifteen to thirty thousand years ago, tamer, less-fearful wolves began to latch onto humans for access to food scraps. These animals, from which our dogs descended, found it easier to beg and search around human dwellings for food rather than exhaustively hunt it down. Sound familiar?

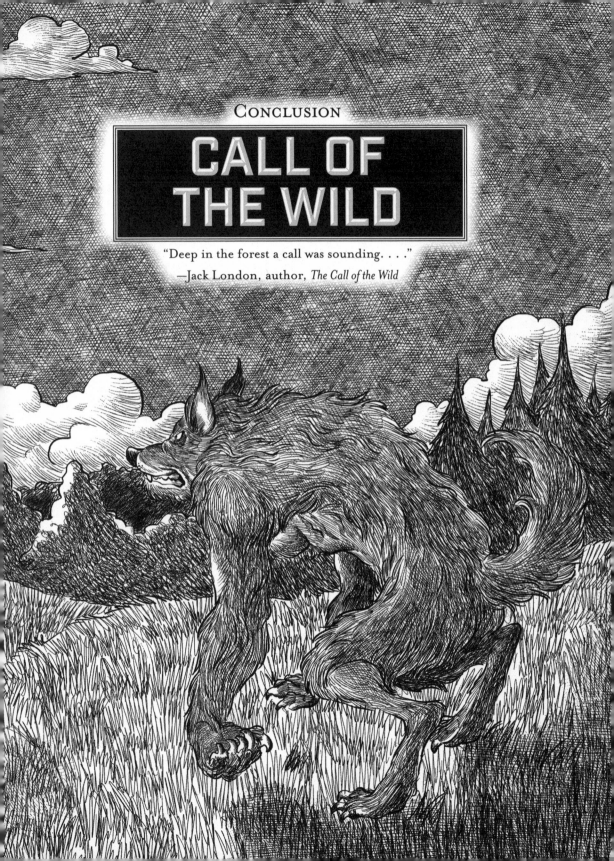

CONCLUSION

CALL OF THE WILD

"Deep in the forest a call was sounding. . . ."
—Jack London, author, *The Call of the Wild*

Like a new moon, there's a tiny sliver of a chance that werewolves exist. Or at least it's fun to think so.

It's easy to see why. These snarling beasties have played a major role in ancient monster legend and lore. And they're still with us, more popular than ever today, appearing in numerous fiction books, films, music, and more.

So why do they have this hold on us? Could they have something to teach us? Maybe it's the power to change and transform that's so appealing—aside from the icky, blood-hungry part, of course! Werewolves show us that changes are possible. That we can maybe turn ourselves into anything we can imagine (as long as it doesn't involve fangs).

Main Sources

Godfrey, Linda S. *Real Wolfmen: True Encounters in Modern America*. New York: TarcherPerigree, 2012.

Guiley, Rosemary Ellen. *The Encyclopedia of Vampires, Werewolves, and Other Monsters*. New York: Checkmark Books, 2004.

Summers, Montague. *The Werewolf in Lore and Legend*. New York: Dover Publications, 2003.

For Further Reading

Curious to learn more about hairy-faced men, women, and kids? If so, then there are numerous titles out there to sink your teeth into. You're probably familiar with fantasy series that feature werewolves, such as Harry Potter's Remus Lupin and Fenrir Greyback. But if you're hungry for more fact-based details, you might check out these books:

Werewolves and Other Shape-Shifters, by Ruth Owen, Bearport Publishing, 2013.

The Girls' Guide to Werewolves: Everything Charming About These Shapeshifters, by Jen Jones, Capstone Press, 2011.

Greatest Movie Monsters: Werewolves, by Daniel E. Harmon, Rosen Central, 2015.

Graphic Mythical Creatures: Werewolves, by Gary Jeffrey, Gareth Stevens Publishing, 2011.

Mysteries, Legends, and Unexplained Phenomena: Werewolves, by Linda S. Godfrey, Checkmark Books, 2008.